PRAISE
THE ONE-HOUR

"Vivid and engaging, this book is full of provocative takeaways. My favorite is takeaway 2: 'Make strategy part of everyone's job.' Now that is something to think about!"

—RICHARD WHITTINGTON, professor of strategic management at the University of Oxford and coauthor of *Exploring Strategy*

"There are bookshelves of strategy books filled with fancy acronyms and models that are useful in understanding strategy and choosing a direction. This book isn't fancy, model-rich, or acronym-ridden; it's dedicated to the practical factors of how to make a strategy work! Great book!"

—ISABELLE PARIZE, chair of Delsey and nonexecutive board member at Coty

"The watershed between strategy and execution is one of today's big problems in strategy. Kraaijenbrink's *The One-Hour Strategy* suggests a way out. Not by simply emphasizing one or the other but by dissolving the distinction and creating one organization-wide approach to strategy."

—HENK W. VOLBERDA, professor of strategy and innovation at the University of Amsterdam and coauthor of *Reinventing Business Models*

"Having read quite a few strategy books, I can definitely say that this book is different. Kraaijenbrink's *One-Hour Strategy* takes strategy out of the stratosphere of the boardroom and brings it down to earth, putting it in the hands of the managers and employees who have to do the actual work."

—RUTGER MILDERS, human resources director at AkzoNobel

"An inspiring read with a refreshingly different outlook compared to other strategy books. Kraaijenbrink offers a practical and powerful approach to engage the entire organization in strategy and help bridge the gap between strategy and execution."

—KATY YOUNG, senior vice president and partner at BTS

"A convincing plea to make everyone in the organization think about strategy regularly, with the frequency increasing with the hierarchical level. Jeroen Kraaijenbrink packages his original message in the form of a smoothly written novel. Not only is his newest book easy to read, but because of its many valuable takeaways and reflection questions, it is also excellent for application in daily practice."

—MARC G. BAAIJ, associate professor of strategic management at Rotterdam School of Management and author of *An Introduction to Management Consultancy*

"*The One-Hour Strategy* is an enjoyable read, challenging the necessity of omnipresent, oversophisticated strategy frameworks. Kraaijenbrink guides readers toward a simple and embracing approach, in which strategy becomes an integral part of people's actual work. Highly recommended."

—HOLGER FEIST, chief strategy officer at Messe München

"Dr. Kraaijenbrink delivers again! Here he leverages decades of experience with helping managers establish and sustain their businesses' strategy conversation. His aim is to show that shaping the business's strategy can become part of everyone's work, an ongoing practice. Part of this is time management, ensuring time is set aside. Part is structure. He carefully builds a structure of takeaways, the questions the business's strategy addresses. Part is Kraaijenbrink's subtlety, the energizing result as individuals throughout the business make their own mark on its strategy. Overall, this is an accessibly written, superbly handy pocketbook for busy people."

—J.-C. SPENDER, research professor at Kozminski
University and author of *Business Strategy*

"*The One-Hour Strategy* presents a new angle on strategy making and challenges traditional strategy perspectives by positioning strategy as part of organizational life rather than an annual activity. Though written in narrative form, with the aim of ensuring accessibility, the concepts are substantial and thought provoking, and the reflective questions useful."

—FRAN ACKERMANN, John Curtin Distinguished Professor at
Curtin Business School and coauthor of *Making Strategy:
Mapping Out Strategic Success*

THE
ONE-HOUR
STRATEGY

THE
ONE-HOUR
STRATEGY

BUILDING A COMPANY OF
STRATEGIC THINKERS

JEROEN KRAAIJENBRINK

**FAST
COMPANY**
Press

Fast Company Press
New York, New York
www.fastcompanypress.com

This work is being published under the Fast Company Press imprint by an exclusive arrangement with *Fast Company*. *Fast Company* and the *Fast Company* logo are registered trademarks of Mansueto Ventures, LLC. The Fast Company Press logo is a wholly owned trademark of Mansueto Ventures, LLC.

Distributed by River Grove Books

Design and composition by Greenleaf Book Group and Brian Phillips
Cover design by Greenleaf Book Group and Brian Phillips

Publisher's Cataloging-in-Publication data is available.

Print ISBN: 978-1-63908-030-4

eBook ISBN: 978-1-63908-031-1

First Edition

CONTENTS

INTRODUCTION

THIS IS A STORY ABOUT MARTIN. He is the new marketing guy at Waters & Flows, and both Martin and Waters & Flows are fictional. But more importantly than anything else, this is a story about strategy, and that part is decidedly real. Not about how strategy is done in the average company today. It's a story about how strategy could, or even should, be done to achieve extraordinary daily success. So it's a bit of a romantic story, too.

To start with a spoiler, the main message is that strategy should become part of the day-to-day processes throughout your organization. All levels, all departments, everyone. It needs to be in your organization's DNA. It should be ordinary, even mundane. Not extraordinary, special, or something reserved for gray people wearing blue suits.

Only then can we expect strategy to become an organization's core competence. And that's what organizations need, especially in a world that is as complex, dynamic, and uncertain as ours today. As they say, the only constant is change. If that is true, a company's ability to spot changes and embrace them in a coherent way is the single most important competence a company can have. Strategy is that competence. Or it should be. And only then can we expect a company to have extraordinary success on an everyday basis.

This is also a story about you and about your organization. Or at least, that is who and what I wrote this book for. Maybe you are Martin; or Alex, the CEO; or Chi, the product manager. Whoever you identify most with, all are a key part of the approach to strategy that unfolds in this book. The approach is called the One-Hour Strategy. I won't give you any more spoilers about why I have called it that. You'll soon find that out when you start reading the story.

As you read this book, I recommend stopping after every chapter, or even after every takeaway, to reflect for a moment on how what you have just read applies to your own organization. To help you with this, every chapter ends with a set of "what is" and "what if" questions. The "what is" questions invite you to evaluate how strategy is currently done at your organization, including the strengths and weaknesses of that effort. The "what if" questions invite you to think about how things could, would, or even should be done differently when adopting the One-Hour Strategy takeaways from the chapter.

Of course, you're not Waters & Flows. But the lessons from

this story are universal. They may require a tweak here and there to make the approach fully fit within your organization. And if your organization is very small or very large, you may need to adjust it a bit more. But the bottom line applies everywhere. Read the story, let it sink in, and turn it into action to make it work for you.

CHAPTER 1

THE SHOCK

5:43 A.M. MARTIN LOOKED AT HIS alarm clock and sighed. *Why do I wake up this early?* he thought. It was Monday, his first day at his new employer, Waters & Flows, and he was excited. But he could have slept for another hour.

He was more excited than he wanted to admit, because he had heard great stories about Waters & Flows. Not so much about the business itself—the company designs, manufactures, installs, and maintains industrial pumps. They do it well and are highly successful. Their products and services are possibly the best and most reliable in the industry. And they're known for how well they treat and care about their employees.

But that's not what the stories were about; at least, those were not the stories that Martin was most interested in. No, the most intriguing stories he had heard were all about how

Waters & Flows is managed—and specifically about how they do strategy.

Martin liked strategy, a lot. While studying for his MBA, he learned about all the different, though largely conventional tools: SWOT, Balanced Scorecard, Five Forces Framework, BCG Matrix, Mission, Vision, Golden Circle, and so on. He was excited to see how Waters & Flows was able to use all these tools effectively and how they had become a master at strategy.

But he didn't have to get up until 7 a.m. *What shall I do?* he pondered. *Get up or try to go back to sleep?* He decided to give it another try and closed his eyes.

* * *

BEEP. BEEP. BEEP. BEEP. BEE— Martin woke up with a shock and smashed the big yellow button on his alarm clock. *What day is it? What time? Did I oversleep!?*

Monday, 7 a.m., he realized. Time to get up. So he stepped out of his bed, took a shower, dressed, and fixed his hair. "You look great," he whispered confidently to the mirror.

After his breakfast, he put on his helmet and jumped on his e-bike, ready for a six-mile commute. Avoiding all the traffic jams that automobiles are prone to, he arrived twenty-five minutes later at Waters & Flows. Time for his first day at his new job!

* * *

His instructions were to go to the front desk and ask for Nina. Outside the office, he locked his e-bike into the shiny steel rack alongside the building, and fixed up his hair with his hands as best he could. He then entered through the sliding doors and approached the reception desk, behind which a young man with dark hair and wearing wire-rimmed glasses stood ready to greet him.

"Hi, I am Martin Koverski. I'm new here, and I was told to ask for Nina."

"Ah, the new guy! Welcome to Waters & Flows. I am Sandeep. Nice to meet you," the man replied. "Just follow me; I'll bring you to Nina. How has your day been going so far?"

Short and pretty chaotic, Martin thought, replying instead, "Um, quite good, I think," as he followed Sandeep up the stairs, stepping briskly.

"Anyway, this is Nina's office," Sandeep said, gesturing with his right hand as they approached the doorway. Then, stepping inside, he said, "Hi, Nina. This is Martin, our newest employee. Can I leave him with you?"

"Sure, Sandeep, thanks. Hi, Martin. I am Nina. I'm the marketing manager of this nice little company."

You call this little? Martin thought as he gazed across the expansive office headquarters. "Hello, Nina, nice to meet you.

And as you know, I am starting today as your new team lead for sales in Asia."

"Of course, and I want to hear all about you. But first, would you like some coffee?"

"I'd love some," Martin replied cheerfully.

. . .

After they both got their cups of coffee from the employee lounge, they returned to Nina's office, and she closed the door behind them. "So we won't be disturbed," she explained with a smile. "Have a seat," she said, as she rounded the desk to her own chair.

"So. Why did you decide to come and work for Waters & Flows?" Nina asked. "Sorry for being so blunt, but I'm always asking this to hear how outsiders see our company—or in your case, newcomers. Because, once you've become an insider, I can't ask you anymore."

"Um . . . ," Martin replied. "Several reasons, of course. You have great products, you work for great customers, your brand stands out from the competition, and I like your company's mission and vision."

"Come on!" Nina laughed. "You can be honest with me. Sure, we're doing pretty good, but we're not exactly Apple, Tesla, or saving the planet, and I can't believe industrial pumps are what fires you up early in the morning."

Okay, Martin thought, *this is going to be interesting.*

"Well, you're probably right, although I do like the fact that you're a sound, profitable company, and I actually do love your products because of how refined they are. But what really got me excited and made me curious are the intriguing things I heard about how your company does strategy."

"Now we're talking! And what intriguing things did you hear?"

"Um, maybe I am completely missing the main point, but I've heard your company is doing strategy in one hour or so . . ."

"Ah, that's what I thought! Another one! Every new hire is asking this. Maybe we should rebrand ourselves as a strategy company instead of an industrial pump maker.

"Are you familiar," Nina continued, "with the mission-vision-SWOT approach?"

Martin nodded slowly.

"And with annual offsites, brown paper, and Post-it sessions?"

"Yes." Martin was wondering where this was going.

"And with trend analysis, extensive strategic planning, and hockey stick curves?"

"That as well. Are you saying you do all of that in one hour?"

"Not at all." Nina smiled. "In fact, we don't do any of that, and certainly not within one hour!"

"But that's what you're supposed to do, right? These are the tools and approaches that I learned, and this is what a large part of my MBA was all about," Martin replied.

"Exactly, and how does all that work out in the real world?

Do you know any company that has successfully applied all these tools to develop and actually implement their strategy?"

"I guess so. Why else would we learn about these tools in business school?"

"Great question. I don't know. Maybe there are companies out there that can make them work, but we certainly can't. That's why we have adopted an entirely different approach. Occasionally, we may use some of those tools, but that's only when a part of our strategy needs some extra attention. It's the exception, not the rule. And what we want is to make strategy the rule, not the exception."

I have to remember that one, Martin thought. *Make strategy the rule, not the exception.* He told himself to make a note after his meeting with Nina.

TAKEAWAY 1

Make strategy the rule, not the exception.

"But how does that work, and how can one possibly do that in one hour?" he asked.

"Let me take you to Marina. She is our One-Hour Strategy specialist. She can tell you all about it. And don't worry, we'll continue our conversation later today. Just knock on my door again after you've talked to Marina. Let me introduce you to her."

"What Is" Questions

1. How does your company currently approach strategy making?

2. How do you (as an individual, or as a manager or employer) presently address strategy making?

3. How successful are your present strategy-making mechanisms? How well is your strategy executed?

4. Are you (or your company) using conventional business methods like SWOT and yearly offsites to design future strategy?

5. How effective have these methodologies been for you? Which shortcomings would you like to overcome?

6. What other, less traditional methodologies have you (or your company) tried to implement?

7. How successful were they, and are you still using them?

"What If" Questions

1. How could your strategy approach be improved? What could make it more effective?

2. What could you do personally to improve how your company makes strategy?

3. What if there were no gap between strategy and execution? How would your company flourish?

4. What would it take to have everyone in the company on board, and committed to the strategy?

5. What would a strategy approach look like in order to effectively deal with the dynamics, complexity, and uncertainty of today's world?

6. What would it require to align your entire company so that everyone's attention goes in the same direction?

7. What benefits would there be if your company were really good at strategy? How would this affect performance and growth?

CHAPTER 2

THE ONE-HOUR RULE

NINA LED MARTIN DOWN the brightly lit corridor, the walls hung with abstract paintings, passing several doors until they arrived at Marina's office. There she knocked three times assertively on the already open door and said, "Hi, Marina. This is Martin, the new Asia marketing guy. Do you have a minute? He wants to learn more about the One-Hour Strategy, and you can explain it far better than me."

"Good morning, Martin. Sure, Nina. I don't have much time at the moment, but I can tell him the gist of it."

"Great! See ya!" and Nina had already left.

Marina stood up and reached out to Martin. "Nice to meet you," she said. "I am Marina, our company's strategy specialist, or chief strategist, or whatever you'd like to call me."

"Nice to meet you, too," Martin replied. "I am Martin . . . the new guy, as Nina said."

"So you want to know more about how we do strategy, right?"

"Yes, I'd love to! I've heard a lot of different things, and I find it quite puzzling so far."

"Okay, let me start with a secret. It is not actually one hour. It's certainly not that we just spend one hour per year on our strategy. Or even one hour per month, for that matter."

"Oh, I see. So what does it mean then?" Martin was getting mixed feelings about Waters & Flows. Had he made the right choice quitting his previous job? Was their strategy approach really so special?

"The core idea is to make strategy the rule, not the exception."

"Nina said exactly the same," Martin responded. "I think I get that, but what does that mean in practice?"

"It means that, in our company, strategy has become part of everyday business. And not just at the executive level but at all levels in the organization."

"You mean that *everyone* in the organization is involved in strategy making?"

"Exactly!"

That's another one I need to write down, Martin thought.

TAKEAWAY 2

Make strategy part of everyone's job.

"But how does that work? People surely can't spend all their time on strategy. They also need to do their actual, day-to-day work, right?"

"Of course. I'll tell you in a minute. But let me first correct you. At our company, strategy *is* part of people's actual work. It is not something on the side. Not something extraordinary. As you heard from Nina, it is the rule, not the exception."

"Okay."

"And can you guess why strategy should be part of everyone's job?"

Martin hesitated, afraid to say the wrong thing. "I don't know; perhaps because everyone knows something and no one knows everything?"

"You're a smart guy. I like that. And you're right. Every single person in our company is an expert in something. Everyone knows, sees, and hears stuff that others don't. They each have unique ideas that no one else does. Not using all that wisdom is almost a crime. And bringing all of that together is our secret sauce."

"Secret sauce?"

"Yes. It's what some call the power of the crowd. It says that the more different perspectives you can bring together, the greater the chance that you'll be on the right track. When you think about it, the traditional top-down approach to strategy is kind of upside-down."

Martin had to think about that one.

"Because," Marina continued, "it involves just a handful of people at the top of the organization in one of the most challenging and complex tasks there is: making strategy. At Waters & Flows, we think the other way around. The more complexity, the more people are involved. Doesn't that sound far more logical?"

"It actually does," Martin replied. *I have to write down this one as well!* he silently continued to himself.

TAKEAWAY 3

When complexity increases, involve more people.

"But doesn't that lead to chaos, politics, and endless discussions?"

"That's what I thought initially as well when I came here nine years ago. But, in fact, the opposite is true. It gives *more* structure, it leads to *less* politics, and it leads to *faster* decisions— and especially to smoother execution."

"How can that be?"

"We've done research on this. Or organizational scientists and psychologists have, but we're relying on their insights. One aspect you already alluded to, when you said nobody knows everything and everybody knows something. By involving people from various levels and positions—and perspectives—you get better and more accurate strategy. It makes your strategy more concrete and realistic, more comprehensive in scope, and thereby easier to execute."

Strategy concrete? Martin felt that another takeaway was coming.

And—*boom*—there it was.

"It may sound counterintuitive, but also in strategy, the devil is in the details. For example, when a company says that their strategy is 'operational excellence' or 'customer intimacy,' they may be right. But it doesn't really say much. The big question is *how* they implement that strategy: what exactly makes them operationally excellent or customer intimate. And that's where the details come in."

TAKEAWAY 4

In making strategy, pay attention to the details.

Now we're talking, Martin thought. *This is getting interesting, and I did make the right choice!*

"But that's not all," Marina continued. "There's a second big reason why involving people from all over the organization in strategy works."

"And that is?"

"It creates ownership. People generally feel committed to something they have helped create and develop and implement. And this greatly facilitates strategy execution. It reduces resistance, and you don't need them to 'buy in' anymore. The strategy is already theirs."

"Makes sense. I felt the same at my old company. We didn't do strategy together, but I always felt most motivated to do my work when I could follow my own plans and when I had a say in deciding our next steps—when I felt that my colleagues and higher-ups actually listened to my ideas."

"I rest my case. I could go on and on. There's a third big reason, but I'll tell you that later, since I don't have much time left. Let me just say for now that, having used this approach for over ten years in our company, I think it is safe to say that it solves virtually all the traditionally persistent problems of strategy and execution. Things like lack of communication, inactivity, lack of focus, resistance, misalignment, and so forth."

"Wow, that really does sound like a secret sauce!"

"I told you."

"I think I am starting to understand why your company is famous for its strategy approach. But," Martin continued, "if you have one more minute, where and how does the one hour come in?"

"Oh, you're right, I completely forgot. Quick then. The core of the One-Hour Rule is that everyone in our company spends one hour of their time on strategy—executives, one hour per day; managers, one hour per week; and employees, one hour per month."

Martin, flabbergasted, wasn't able to speak.

"Here it is written down." Marina pointed at an etched glass plaque on her wall. "Everyone has this in their office or at their work station."

THE ONE-HOUR RULE

Executives spend one hour per day,
managers spend one hour per week, and
employees spend one hour per month
on strategy.

"I have to run," Marina gestured at the glass door as she spoke, "but I see Alex's meeting has ended early. She's our CEO, and I bet she would like to meet you and tell you more. Let me take you to her office."

Martin smiled. He had made the right decision.

"What Is" Questions

1. Who is presently making strategy in your company? How well does that work?

2. Who is not involved and what is the effect of that on your strategy and on execution?

3. How many people in your company truly understand the company's strategy?

4. And how many are able and motivated to implement it as intended?

5. To what extent is your company's strategy concrete and actionable?

6. How much effective time do people—executives, managers, and employees—spend on strategy throughout the year?

7. How is your strategy kept alive and up to date so that it keeps on driving the day-to-day work?

"What If" Questions

1. Are there strategic choices in your company that are so simple that they can be left to the leadership team only? Are there strategic choices that are not that simple?

2. What do you believe would be the benefits for your company if all employees would be effectively involved in the strategy-making process?

3. What would be the benefits for employees? How would it affect their engagement and work motivation?

4. And what about you? How would this benefit you personally?

5. How would it help your company if people talked about strategy on a regular (daily, weekly, monthly) basis instead of once every couple of years?

6. As a percentage, how much more effective would you estimate the strategy process would be? Why?

7. How would the execution of your company's strategy improve if your strategy were concrete and detailed, yet viewed persistently as an ongoing "work in progress"?

CHAPTER 3

THE ONE-HOUR STRATEGY EXECUTIVE

MARINA KNOCKED ON ALEX'S DOOR. "Sorry to interrupt, but I saw Julia leave early. Do you have a moment to meet Martin? He is our new sales guy, and he got confused about our One-Hour Rule. I'm running late for a meeting. Can you tell him more?"

Well, Martin thought, *I am not really confused, and I certainly don't want you saying such a thing to the CEO.*

"Sure. Nice to meet you, Martin."

"I have to run!" Marina shouted over her shoulder and left.

"Good morning, Mrs. Adams. My name is Martin Koverski. It is a real pleasure and honor to meet you," Martin started.

"Ha ha, please stop being so formal. I'm Alex."

Martin shook her hand.

"How do you like your new job so far?" she asked.

Martin didn't know what to say. He hadn't even started yet.

"I'm still trying to find my way and meet some people, but so far, it looks very promising."

"Why? What makes it look promising?"

"I mean . . ." Martin stumbled, thinking, *Are they all this direct?* "I haven't really started yet with my actual work, but what Nina and Marina told me about the One-Hour Strategy sounds very promising."

"Aha! But then you already know that this is part of your 'actual work,'" Alex said, using air quotes.

"You're right. I also learned that here at Waters & Flows, everyone is involved in strategy and that people must spend one hour per day, week, or month on strategy—depending on their position, that is. Marina said you could tell me more about that."

"I certainly can, but I only will tell you my part of the story—the one hour per day for executives. For the other parts, you need to ask our managers and employees. They are the experts in what they do."

"I certainly will. Thank you for being so generous with your time."

"Oh, stop being so formal! I love explaining this. Please close the door so that no one comes in to bother us with less interesting stuff."

After closing the door, Martin took the seat across Alex's desk.

"All right, let me explain. The basic rule is very simple. Every executive spends one hour per day on strategy. It could be more but not less."

"You mean *every* day?"

"Every day. Or at least, every working day. I do have my week-ends, and my partner would kill me if I worked all weekend."

"Isn't that a lot of time, and don't you have other things to do?"

"No and yes. Like any CEO, I do have plenty of other things to do. But I don't think spending one hour per day on strategy is a lot. It's about 10 percent of my time."

"I suppose if you put it like that . . ."

"It is like that. As CEO, I think my primary responsibility at this company is making sure that we're following the right strategy and actually delivering on it. Other tasks are important too, but they are secondary."

"Makes sense," Martin confirmed.

"And," Alex continued, "this applies to all executives in our company, so it applies across the board. They all spend at least one hour per day on our strategy."

"Okay, I get the 10 percent idea and that everyone across your executive team spends a significant amount of time on strategy. But why on a daily basis? Doesn't that make the whole approach very fragmented?"

"On the contrary! You may think so, because, after all, what can you do in one hour? But the whole point is to do it every day so that strategy becomes second nature, a normal and integral part of your job. And instead of being fragmented, this makes it a continuous process that never stops—or starts."

Another takeaway! Martin thought.

> **TAKEAWAY 5**
>
> Make strategy a continuous process, not an event.

"And this is also how you make strategy the rule, not the exception, right?"

"Exactly. And the main advantage of this is that there is continuous follow-up and progress. Until ten years ago, we still did it the traditional way. Every year we organized a two-day event at a nice resort. We spent the morning on some serious work using SWOT, Post-its, and so on. And in the afternoon, we did team building."

"That's how my previous employer did it as well," Martin said.

"These events were exciting and energizing. The big problem with them, though, was that afterward, everyone went back to work, and nothing really happened."

"You know, that was my experience as well!"

"Therefore, we decided to do it very differently. Instead of organizing annual events at a nice hotel or resort, we took strategy literally back inside our company, to our own offices and meeting rooms. Because only then can you make it a normal part of everyone's work. And only then can you be truly focused on your company's strategy rather than being distracted by the new and unfamiliar environment."

Martin took his notebook from his bag. "Sorry, but I have to write something down. I've gotten so many takeaways already that I won't remember all of them."

"Of course. Take your time. I'll get you another coffee. Black?"

"A bit of sugar, thanks."

TAKEAWAY 6

Make strategy internally,
within your own offices and meeting rooms.

After jotting down this latest takeaway, Martin closed his notebook just as Alex returned with two cups of coffee.

"Thanks. Can I ask you one more question?"

"Sure. I still have a couple of minutes."

"I agree with everything you're saying, but I really wonder *how* you do this. What do you do during the hour? How exactly do you spend your time?"

"Great question. I can tell you half of the story. The other half you need to ask Chi about. He's our product manager and was involved in conceptualizing and developing the whole one-hour approach."

"I think I have an appointment with him tomorrow morning anyway. Let me have a look—Chi Wang, right?"

"That's him. I'll tell you the simplest part, and he can tell you the rest. Now, here's what I do. Every day I spend the dedicated one hour working on three key questions. I wrote them down here." Alex showed Martin a simple sheet of paper, on which neatly typed appeared the following:

THE THREE QS: RPM

Q1: Relevance. Do we still have the right strategy?

Q2: Progress. Did we make the right progress?

Q3: Mood. Is everyone still on board?

Alex explained, "The first question is all about calibrating our strategy. Both our company and the rest of the world are constantly moving. This means we have to continuously keep track of internal and external changes—and adjust or modify those parts of our strategy that are no longer relevant in the new or emerging situation."

"Does this mean you are constantly changing the strategy? Isn't the whole idea that strategy gives a company stability and direction?"

"You're very right. Strategy most certainly provides us direction and a stable reference point in this rapidly changing world.

This is why I always say, 'Monitor actively; change reluctantly.' You may want to write that down," she added, smiling.

TAKEAWAY 7

Monitor actively; change reluctantly.

"What I mean is that I am very keen on keeping abreast of any changes within and outside our organization. So, for example, I want to know if there are any new technologies coming up, what our competitors are doing, if there are any new industry regulations coming from the government, and so on. But also, I want to know which new employees have come in, how our inventory is doing, and any other internal development that may be going on. The same for everyone else in our company. We all have our antennas out to capture any signals of imminent change that may affect our industry or organization and require changes to our strategy."

"Seems the right thing to do nowadays."

"Yes, and at the same time, we try to limit the actual changes we make to our strategy—exactly for the reason you mentioned."

"I can follow that. Does that also mean you don't formally develop a new strategy every three to five years? That you adjust it part by part, as a continuous process?"

"That's right. Quite a change in perspective, isn't it?"

"Yes, but now as I think about it, this looks a lot like what I know from quality management—continuous improvement, PDCA, total quality management, and so on. There, the idea is also to continuously make improvements. And also that everyone in the organization must be involved."

"That's exactly where the whole One-Hour Strategy idea comes from. What applies to quality management applies to strategy as well."

"I probably need to learn a bit more about the one-hour approach to see how this really works in practice, but I certainly believe you."

"Great. Now let me quickly explain the second and third question, because my next meeting starts in five minutes."

"Yes, please!"

"The second question focuses on progress and is really basic project management. To ensure we make sufficient progress with the execution of our strategy, I focus every day on a specific part of our strategy and evaluate whether we're doing the right things or whether we need to initiate new actions. And once we can cross off an initiative from the list—ideally because it's been accomplished—I'll make sure to add a new one, so that we keep on moving forward."

"I get it."

"The last question, regarding mood, is a tricky one. The first focuses on the strategy we have in mind. The second question focuses on action and results—execution. But the last one is super important, too. The heart of our company—and any organization—is our people. And, while we still may have the perfect strategy, and may be perfectly on schedule executing it, we must keep track of how our people think about it. Are they still motivated? Are they committed? Or are there signals that some people might be losing connection with our strategy or company? If so, we want to know ASAP."

"Very interesting, and you're completely right. I hadn't thought about that part. And no one taught us that during my MBA studies. But this was one of the reasons I left Brick & Co., my previous employer. Business-wise we were doing great, but people were quite demotivated, and there was a lot of gossip and silent resistance. But let me not say too much about that. Thanks a lot. I believe you need to go?"

"I do, thanks, but I really wanted to explain this last part to you as well. In any case, as I said, Chi can tell you much more about the finer details. It was nice meeting you, and welcome to Waters & Flows! I think you're going to do terrifically well here!"

"Thank you, ma'am." Alex frowned about the formalism, while Martin took his notebook and thanked her for the time spent talking to him.

Martin diligently spent the rest of the day working in the marketing department, familiarizing himself with the Waters & Flows approach, talking to his new colleagues, and getting started with his first project. Or, on doing his "actual work," as he had called it himself.

SELF-EVALUATION

"What Is" Questions

1. How often does your company actively work on its strategy—once a year, every three years, every five years? Ever?

2. Where does strategy making typically take place—offsite at a hotel, a resort, or elsewhere? What are the upsides and downsides of that?

3. If your company redefines or redesigns its strategy on a yearly basis or less often, how "alive" and actualized is the most recent strategy at present? Is it still sufficiently driving day-to-day business?

4. To what extent is the implementation of this strategy progressing according to plan? Do you actually know how far your strategic progress has advanced to date?

5. Is the strategy regularly checked, revisited, or updated? If not, what is the effect of that?

6. To what extent are employees truly on board and motivated to execute the strategy?

7. How much time do your company's executives spend on strategy per day or week? Is that enough?

"What If" Questions

1. What upsides can you see if strategy were to be effectively embedded in the company's day-to-day operations?

2. What would be the effect on your strategy if people throughout your company shared relevant developments with others on a regular basis?

3. What would be the effect on execution if people throughout your company were continuously focused on the company's strategy?

4. How well would your strategy perform if relevance, progress, and mood were effectively managed throughout the year?

5. What do you believe would be the benefits of making strategy within the offices and meeting rooms of the company?

6. What would happen to your strategy and execution if executives in your company paid attention to it every day?

7. What would your company look like if strategy and execution were part of everyday work? How would that be different from the way the company operates today?

CHAPTER 4

THE ONE-HOUR STRATEGY MANAGER

THE NEXT MORNING MARTIN was abruptly awakened by his blaring 7 a.m. alarm. He had woken up at least three times during the night, each time finding himself in the middle of a bizarrely animated dream about a big, loud, old-fashioned alarm clock. The really odd thing about the clock in his dreams was that it had the numeral "1" every place where the other face numbers should have been. Apparently—or so Martin took it to mean—he had to process all the new stuff he had learned about on his first day on the job, and particularly this intriguing one-hour idea.

Today, first thing in the morning, he would have a meeting with Chi, the product manager. He couldn't wait. What Alex had told him was fascinating. And at the executive level, it made sense to him. But how would this work for the company's managers? Would their approach to the One-Hour Strategy be the same?

After his morning routine and e-bike commute, he arrived at Waters & Flows at 8:30 a.m. sharp, right on time for his meeting with Chi.

"Good morning, Sandeep," he greeted when he entered the building.

"Good morning, new guy!" Sandeep smiled.

"I have a meeting with Chi. His office is on the second floor, right?"

"Indeed, room 221."

"Thanks, and have a nice day!"

Sandeep waved at him.

Martin went to room 221. The door was open, but no one was there. Not knowing what to do, he decided to enter and take a seat. After all, they were colleagues, so Chi wouldn't mind, right?

Three minutes later, Chi came in, fully lost in thought and whistling a faintly familiar melody.

"Goodness! You scared me!" Chi half-shouted when he saw Martin.

"Oh, sorry! I thought—it's probably impolite, but—I didn't see you, and we have an appointment."

"No worries. I just didn't see you. You must be Martin then. Hi, I am Chi."

"I'm indeed Martin. Nice to meet you."

"Please refresh my memory: What were we going to talk about?" Chi said.

"Well, a couple of things, mostly about how you see our products and what you think of the way we currently market them. But, before that, if you'll allow me, I'd like to ask you about the One-Hour Strategy thing. Would you mind?"

"Not at all. I love to talk about that. I can even proudly say that I've been one of the creators of the one-hour method. So ask whatever you want."

"Thanks. Part of it I already know. Yesterday, I spoke to Nina, Marina, and Alex, and they've told me quite a bit. But Alex also mentioned that you could tell me much more."

"What do you already know then?"

"Let's see, I know about the one hour per day, week, and month. And about making strategy the excepti—no, the rule, not the exception. And that everyone is involved. Oh, and also about the three questions: relevance, progress, and mood."

"Then you already know quite a bit."

"I think so, but I'm especially curious about two things. Alex told me that there are more details to the hour than just the three questions. That's one. The other thing is that I don't understand how all of this works for managers. If I'm correct, you spend one hour per week on strategy, but how does that work?"

"Perfect. I'll start with the first. I think you mean our 6M Model."

"Could be. Alex didn't say what it was."

"I'm sure that's what she meant. She always refers the new ones to me to explain that part of our method. I think you also have heard that we believe that strategy is all about details. Or at least, it is significantly about the details," Chi continued.

"Uh-huh."

"Well, to work on the details of strategy, and at the same time keep the overview in mind, we have developed a simple tool. Most people call it the 6M Model, but I like to call it the MMMMMM Model."

"Mmm . . . ," Martin pondered.

"Indeed, MMMMMM. But anyway, let's simply call it the 6M Model, since that's the official name. It stands for the six elements of strategy: Magic, Market, Means, Money, Meaning, and Momentum."

"Magic? Okay, that sounds fascinating. Can you tell me what they mean?"

"Of course, that's where I was heading. But instead of telling you, let me show you how the six elements are defined. Where is it?" Chi was digging into various piles of paper on his desk. *Not exactly an organized or paperless office*, Martin observed quietly.

"Sorry for the mess, but I found it. Here, take a look." Chi showed Martin a sheet of paper with six bullets:

THE SIX MS OF STRATEGY

M1: Magic.
The products and services that we offer and what they do for our customers.

M2: Market.
The customers whose needs we serve and the alternatives we compete against.

M3: Means.
The assets and capabilities that we and our partners can bring to the table.

M4: Money.
The way and amount of revenues we generate versus the costs and risks we have.

M5: Meaning.
The things that we find most important and to which we most aspire.

M6: Momentum.
The factors outside our control that help or hinder us in what we do.

"Wow, that's a useful list! I wish I'd had that when I was studying for my MBA. Could have saved me a lot of work. It's quite elegant. Looks pretty complete to me but also simple to use."

"That is the whole point. We wanted something complete so that you don't forget about any key element. But we also wanted it to be as simple as possible. After all, there's only so much you can do in an hour!"

"And how *do* you use this?" Martin asked. "Wait, I think I already get it. When you combine this with the three questions, you get a pretty powerful tool where you ask about the relevance, progress, and mood for each of the six Ms. Am I correct?"

"Spot on. Now you know the secret of our One-Hour Strategy method."

"That's exciting. I knew I made the right choice to come and work for Waters & Flows!"

"I could tell you in some more detail how this works, but first I want to show you one more illustration. You know, the 6Ms are great, but we've also gone one step further. We've created a simple 'canvas,' a kind of schematic that contains all six on a single sheet of paper in a logically and visually structured way. Here is what I mean." Chi showed the following.

The 6M Model

MONEY

MEANS

MAGIC

MARKET

MEANING

MOMENTUM

"This is great." Martin kept on looking at the canvas. "It really makes sense how the 6Ms are organized. On the left side, there's supply; on the right side, demand; and in the middle, the products and services that connect them."

"Indeed, that's the horizontal part. And vertically, the Magic element connects doing something meaningful with making money, or profitability, if you will. And all around it is the context in which we operate, and that defines the Momentum."

"Can I get a copy of this?" Martin asked eagerly.

"Sure, take this one; I've got plenty of copies."

"Thanks. This more than answers my first question. It gives me something to chew on. I didn't think about this earlier, but since everyone in the company uses it, I suppose I will be using it, too?"

"There's no way around it. You will start dreaming and breathing it—for more than just one hour." Martin suddenly remembered the strange clock dream he'd experienced the previous night. *Wow*, he thought, *it's like I've already begun to assimilate it!*

"Can't wait," Martin said, smiling. "That brings me to the second question I had."

"Which was again . . . ?"

"How you or other managers are using this. From Alex I learned she is spending an hour on this every day. But how does it work in your case, when you do this one hour per week?"

"Basically, very much the same as Alex, only less often."

"What do you mean? If, as an executive, she needs one hour per day, how can you do the same in one hour per week?"

"I don't."

"Uh, but isn't that what you just told me?"

"Sort of, but the main difference is that I don't necessarily do things the same way Alex does, or as anyone else, for that matter. She has her responsibilities, I have mine, and so does everyone else in our company. The point is that you use the one hour, and these tools, and you apply them to your own situation and responsibilities and your own specific challenges."

"Okay, so . . . ?" Martin felt another takeaway coming.

"Everyone works at strategy from their own perspective. At the executive level, someone like Alex looks at the 6Ms for our entire company. I, and other managers, though, look at the 6Ms as they are relevant to each of our own jobs or departments and each based on our own expertise and experience."

> ### TAKEAWAY 8
> Everyone works at strategy at their own level
> and from their own perspective.

"For example, for me as product manager, the M for Means is about the production-related assets and capabilities our company has. And when I look at our partners in the supply chain, I do this from a production perspective. Your manager, Nina, does the same, but from a marketing perspective. She looks at the marketing assets and capabilities our company has and which companies we partner with for that.

"The same for the other Ms," Chi continued. "When I look at the market, I look at what competitors do in terms of production and how we can improve our production to better serve our customers. In this same way, every department looks at the 6Ms from their perspective. IT looks at IT, finance at finance, HR at HR, and so on."

"And what about the three satellite locations of Waters & Flows?"

"Same there. Of course, they have to work within the boundaries of the corporate strategy and the functional strategies that we develop here at headquarters. But, within those boundaries, they also use the 6M Model to look at their local market, their local means, their local cost structure, and so on."

"And because you're all using exactly the same questions and model, it all adds up to the company's overall strategy?"

"If we do it well, yes. That's the aim. In this way we create alignment across all departments, levels, and locations of our company. Of course, we can always improve, but this methodology has radically improved the way our company works. We have better communication, fewer silos, more focus, and more collaboration. And that leads to better processes, better products, and a more satisfied customer. As a result, we make more money—and most importantly, we create more value for all our key stakeholders. It's a win-win-win-win—I don't know how many wins, but you get the point."

"I certainly do!" Martin's brain was steaming. He needed a break, even though he still had a lot of questions. Also, they had used the entire meeting time to talk about strategy. He estimated he could bear the answer to one last question.

"I realize we didn't talk about the main reason I came to you—what you think about the way we currently market our products."

"That can wait. This was much more important. Once you understand the one-hour method, everything you hear will be easier to connect and align anyway. So we've spent our time well."

"I have a final question about the one hour, and then I'll leave you alone."

"Sure."

"Why do managers spend one hour per week while executives spend one hour per day?"

"Two reasons. First, I only have to look at one perspective—production—which is much simpler than their job: looking at how all of it adds up at the company level, from my department along with every other department. Second, the executive board's primary responsibility is strategy. For me, it is important but not my primary responsibility. Therefore, I still spend time on it every week but not as intensively as they must do."

"Perfect. Thank you very much for all of this."

"You're welcome. To get the full picture, though, you also need to talk to one of our employees, or, perhaps even better, a few of them to get a broad perspective. I'm sure you'll find it insightful to see how, also at that level, our people are intimately involved in our company's strategy."

"Tomorrow, I have my work-from-home day, and I've scheduled some video calls with people from both our marketing department and HR. I'll ask them."

Like the previous day, the rest of Martin's second day at

Waters & Flows was devoted to doing his "actual work." He talked to some customers, analyzed the company's sales pipeline, and already identified some potential points for improvement.

SELF-EVALUATION

"What Is" Questions

1. What, precisely, does the word "strategy" mean within your company? How well do people understand and agree on what strategy is, and what the purpose of strategy truly is?

2. What specific strategy models or tools, if any, are used within your company to help make strategy concrete and tangible?

3. How much time do (mid-level) managers in your company spend on strategy per week? Is that enough?

4. If and when they spend time on strategy, how do they do so? Are they doing the right thing, and is it effective? What can be improved?

5. Is your company's strategy complete? Does it address everything that it should address?

6. Is your company's strategy concrete? Is the meaning behind your company's strategy clear and tangible, including what needs to be done to achieve it?

7. Does the company's strategy effectively cascade to lower levels? Is there a similar mechanism for allowing innovative strategy making to percolate from lower operational levels up to management and even to executives?

"What If" Questions

1. What would be the effect of having one simple strategy framework that is used across the entire company?

2. How would this help to create alignment across business units, divisions, departments, and levels? How would it facilitate both top-down and bottom-up communication?

3. What do you believe would happen if all managers were actively engaged in strategy making and execution every week?

4. How would your company's performance be affected if everyone could contribute to strategy from their own unique role or perspective?

5. How would your company perform if all six Ms—Magic, Market, Means, Money, Meaning, and Momentum—were specified and in sync?

6. How would you personally use the 6M Model to monitor and manage your strategy in your specific role in the company?

7. Which immediate points for improvement can you identify when you look at the six Ms from your role in the company? What might you be able to do most effectively, immediately or in the short term?

CHAPTER 5

THE ONE-HOUR STRATEGY EMPLOYEE

TODAY, MARTIN HAD HIS working-from-home day. This was ideal, because he could easily talk to a couple of employees from each of all three locations without having to travel. And it was raining as well, so not having to bike to work was another advantage.

Martin was up and ready early. His first meeting was scheduled for 9 a.m., but because he didn't have to make his commute, he had some free time before the meeting. It was 8:10, he'd already had his coffee, and to his surprise and delight, his new laptop worked at once.

He decided to have another look at the 6M Model.

"Means, Magic, Market," he mumbled while drawing a horizontal line with his finger. "It really does make sense. If you're doing it right, your products and services are the magic that connects your means to the market."

"And Money, Magic, Meaning," he said, drawing a vertical line, "makes sense too. You again need the magic of the right products and services to make money and be meaningful."

"Even Momentum makes sense. Because that's what opportunities and threats really do: they either accelerate what you do or slow it down. Pretty smart people there at Waters & Flows," he mused.

* * *

At 8:56, he saw on-screen that Gunther, one of Waters & Flows' account representatives and the first person he would meet today, had started the video call already. Martin connected.

"Hello, Gunther, can you hear me? I can't see you yet."

"Wait . . . yes, let me put on my camera. Where is it . . . yes, right, why . . . ? Oh. Now it should work, right?"

"Yes, it does. Can you see me as well?"

"Definitely. Hello, nice to meet you. I'm Gunther."

"Hi, I am Martin, the new marketing guy. I've joined your department this week. I don't think I've seen you at the office, correct?"

"Correct. I've been traveling, and I'm actually visiting one of our clients at the moment. Important sales meeting later today."

"Sounds good. And that's the main topic I'd like to learn

about in our meeting today: how you guys conduct sales meetings with existing clients. In an hour I talk to Michelle about the sales funnel for new prospects."

"Michelle Dubois? Good luck." Gunther smiled.

"Well, thanks, but why do you say that, if you don't mind my asking?"

"You'll find out. She's quite a character. Don't get me wrong—she's great at what she does, but she just doesn't accept no."

"Okay, thanks for the warning, I guess."

"Regarding our meeting," Martin continued, "there's one thing I'd like to ask you before we move to sales."

"Sure."

"You probably can guess it, but I'm learning about our company's one-hour approach to strategy. So far, I've learned the highlights and how executives and managers apply it one hour per day and per week, respectively. But I don't understand yet how it works at the employee level. Can you explain?"

"So, you want to know our secret sauce?"

"Is it really that secret?"

"Not at all. Just kidding. We're shouting it from the rooftops, so it's not a secret at all. What do you want to know?"

"I understand the idea that every employee spends one hour per month on strategy. I also know the 6M Model and the three RPM questions of Relevance, Progress, and Mood. But I'm not real clear about how you can work with these tools or concepts one hour per month."

"And yet that's what we do. Or at least, I do. Whether it's actually one hour per month I don't know; I don't count the minutes. But the point is that everyone thinks about strategy from their own level and perspective in a kind of continuous way."

It looks like the one-hour approach is really embraced and understood by everyone! Martin thought. "Uh-huh," he said.

"We do this in two ways," Gunther continued. "First, and most importantly, every employee is asked to keep the 6Ms and the three questions always front of mind. While working, but also while reading the news, watching television, working out, and so on."

"Isn't that a lot of work and extremely tiring?"

"Not at all. Once you understand the model and questions, and you have internalized them, it becomes second nature. You can't switch it off anymore."

Martin looked at the list of takeaways he had written down over the past two days and asked, "So this is the way you make strategy part of everyone's day-to-day job, how you monitor actively, and how strategy creation becomes a continuous process rather than a single event?"

"You've been paying attention, sir!"

Martin blushed. "Well, I've been taking some notes, and I thought these were important takeaways. But I am going to add this one." He wrote:

TAKEAWAY 9

Internalize the 6M Model and the three questions
and keep them front of mind, always.

"What did you write down?"

Martin showed it in front of the camera.

"Perfect. That's what I meant," Gunther said, nodding enthusiastically.

"Now that I think of it," Martin asked, "does this apply only to employees or also to managers and executives?"

"To everyone in the company. That's why it works. When it concerns our strategy, everyone's attention is focused on the same six elements and the same three questions. There's a lot of stuff that doesn't work at Waters & Flows—or at least as well as we'd like—but this works very well."

"Great. And the second way?"

"What do you mean?" Gunther looked puzzled.

"You said there were two ways that employees spend one hour per month."

"Ah, of course. Yes, the second way is more formal and more an actual hour. Once a month we have a one-hour Strategy Dialogue with everyone in the marketing department."

"Dialogue?"

"Yes. We call it a dialogue to stress the purpose and atmosphere of the meeting: an open and safe dialogue where people can feel free to share what's on their minds. Not a discussion with verbal fights between opposing camps but a constructive dialogue focused on improving our strategy."

Martin nodded.

"During the meeting, our manager, Nina, who I think you have met—"

"Yes."

"Nina leads an interactive dialogue along the lines of the 6Ms and the three questions. The point of that workshop, or dialogue, is that all of us bring in what we call our 3Is—our Issues, Insights, and Ideas—which we employ as inputs for the 6Ms."

"Interesting. Why Issues, Insights, and Ideas?"

"Let me share my screen. Wait . . . yes, this is the right one. Here are the 3Is. Can you see them?" Gunther showed a slide with the 3Is explained:

3I INPUTS FOR THE STRATEGY DIALOGUE

I1: **Issues.** Any problem, bottleneck, or mistake that you have identified since the last strategy meeting.

I2: Insights. Any fact, observation, or experience that you learned since the last strategy meeting.

I3: Ideas. Any solution, improvement, or innovation that you identified since the last strategy meeting.

He went on. "We particularly emphasize that any 'I' can be very small. The goal is not to come up with grand or disruptive issues, insights, or ideas. Similar to the idea of continuous improvement, the point is that there is a continuous flow of incremental steps to constantly hone and improve our strategy. But, at the same time, *anything* that you can bring in is of added value, no matter how insignificant, crazy, or inappropriate you think it is."

"So they really want to lower the threshold so that everyone feels free to bring in what they want?"

"Right."

"Okay, let me check whether I get it right with the 6Ms, 3Qs, and 3Is. . . . Oh no, but how do the three questions come in?"

"Let me show you another slide, outlining the standard agenda for our strategy meetings. Wait . . . here it is. Can you see it?"

"Yes."

AGENDA FOR THE MONTHLY
ONE-HOUR STRATEGY DIALOGUE

2 min. Welcome by the manager: check if everyone is present and, if not, why.

10 min. Mood check: Is everyone still on board? Any Issues, Insights, or Ideas?

20 min. Progress check 6Ms: Did we make the right progress? Any Issues, Insights, or Ideas?

20 min. Relevance check 6Ms: Do we still have the right strategy? Any Issues, Insights, or Ideas?

8 min. Closure, action points, and anything else that needs to be said.

"As you see, we first make sure everyone from our department is there. This is a mandatory meeting. Of course, it could happen that someone isn't there, but it should always be clear why. We're very strict on this."

"I suppose otherwise people might skip it if they think they have more urgent issues to deal with."

"You're 100 percent correct. Ironic, don't you think, in a

company that puts so much emphasis on strategy? But it happens. Anyway, the discipline is there now, but we have to work to maintain it. A must for making strategy second nature is that you never let something else get in the way. Even though working on your strategy may not be urgent, it is important, especially in the long run."

Hearing "urgent" and "important," Martin remembered the Eisenhower Matrix that he had learned about during his MBA studies. Finally, something he recognized!

"After that," Gunther continued, "we focus on mood. We want to know how people feel, whether there are any frustrations or signs of disengagement, and whether people still believe in the current strategy. We do this first, because emotions tend to get in the way of everything else. If we were to start with progress or relevance, there could remain an elephant in the room that completely disturbs the dialogue. Usually, we don't need the full ten minutes for that because most people will already have shared their concerns with Nina during the month. But sometimes this becomes the main part of the meeting."

"I see." Martin nodded again. "And the rest of the time you split equally between progress and relevance."

"You're right. Of course, how much time we spend exactly on each topic differs between meetings, but this is the idea. This gives us about three minutes for each of the 6Ms for both progress and relevance."

"Isn't that short?"

"It is. But you have to realize that the point of the meeting is to get things on the table, not to discuss or debate them at length. You can think of it as a brainstorming session in which each individual's issues, insights, and ideas are inventoried. Any more in-depth discussion that might be warranted will take place later, outside the dialogue sessions."

"I actually have a question about that. How does that work in practice?"

"It's like any other brown paper, Post-it, or whiteboard session. Nina asks, we talk, and she writes down the issues, insights, and ideas that we bring in. We use a whiteboard, but I know other departments are using flip-overs or brown paper. And the IT department has fully digitalized it."

"Of course!" Martin smiled.

"So," Gunther added, "if you have an idea about, let's say, a new market segment, you bring it in when we talk about the market element. And if I see an issue with our CRM system, I bring it in when we talk about our means. And so on. Quite simple actually, once you get the hang of it."

"It sure is. It makes me wonder why every other organization isn't doing it this way."

"No idea. Apparently, the old-fashioned paradigm is so deeply rooted in how people think strategy should be done that changing that is difficult."

"To say the least! Take my MBA. I've never heard or read anything like this during the entire program. The only thing I could recognize was the Eisenhower Matrix when you talked about urgency and importance."

"Oh. Did I? Anyway, it just makes sense to do it this way."

For the rest of the hour, Martin and Gunther spoke about the company's sales approach with existing clients. Martin was surprised how operational their sales approach was. He had read that one of the company's strategic goals was to become more of a strategic partner for their customers so that Waters & Flows would not only sell and service pumps but also advise customers on the choice and design of the entire infrastructure in which the pumps were going to be used. But Gunther had not spoken about that at all. Drawing from his previous job, Martin immediately had an idea that he could bring in during the next Strategy Dialogue. As he had experienced there, achieving the company's goal would require a change in who the actual customer—the person—was that Waters & Flows should be talking to. Next to the purchasing department, they would also have to speak directly with the customer's process engineers. He made a mental note of that.

SELF-EVALUATION

"What Is" Questions

1. How would you characterize your employees' general attitude toward strategy in your company? Do they see it as something they are responsible for?

2. To what extent are employees in your company truly involved in strategy making?

3. Why not more? What keeps you or your company from involving them more actively in the creation of new strategy?

4. If any, how actively are you capturing the issues, insights, and ideas that employees have regarding the company's strategy?

5. How much time per month or year do employees in your company spend on strategizing? When and how divided over the year is that?

6. Which mechanisms are you using to involve employees in strategy making? How well do these work?

7. What have you done personally to get involved in the company's strategy making and/or to involve others?

"What If" Questions

1. What would happen if your employees would share the issues, insights, and ideas they have regarding your company's strategy on a regular basis?

2. How could you effectively harness and integrate these issues, insights, and ideas into the company's strategy process?

3. How would that benefit your company's performance?

4. How would it benefit your employees and their engagement?

5. What do you believe would be the effect of having monthly Strategy Dialogue sessions in all departments?

6. How would you practically organize such sessions? Consider such issues as: Where would you hold such sessions? Would they be standing or sitting, physical or digital, highly structured, or more open?

7. How would you make sure that every employee who is your responsibility has the 3Is and 6Ms front of mind?

CHAPTER 6

ONE-HOUR STRATEGY FUNDAMENTALS

THE REST OF THE WEEK, Martin didn't talk much about the one-hour method. He got to know his colleagues in marketing better and met a lot of people. He liked the people he met. Michelle was indeed a bit of a character, as Gunther had said, but she was very smart and truly caring about the quality of work. In fact, she was so dedicated to her work on the company's sales funnel that she hadn't given Martin the chance to talk about the One-Hour Strategy at all. While everything was quite new, he was already starting to feel at home at Waters & Flows.

On Wednesday, halfway through his second week, he was getting second thoughts, though. Not so much about Waters & Flows itself, or about his colleagues, but about the One-Hour Strategy approach. Was it really that great? Did it work as smoothly as it seemed, or were there issues as well?

There must be, he thought. *Nothing is ever ideal or perfect, especially in a chaotically evolving business and commerce world.* He decided to ask Marina. As the one-hour expert, she should definitely know all the details, including the more challenging parts.

After lunch he knocked on her door. "Hi, Marina. Do you have a few minutes?"

"Of course, Martin, come in." Martin closed the door and took the seat in front of Marina's desk.

"How can I help you? I bet it is about the One-Hour Strategy. How do you like it?"

"Um, very much, but that's indeed what I wanted to ask you about. It all sounds great, but I am still wondering: Does it really work that well in practice? Aren't there any issues? I'm asking because I learned in business school that failure rates in strategy are extremely high. If I remember correctly, 50 to 70 percent of strategies fail to be executed. And there are major problems, like lack of communication, a too-rigid strategy, conflicting priorities, failure of buy-in by employees, and so forth."

"So you're asking about the dark sides of the One-Hour Strategy," Marina interrupted him.

"Dark? Maybe not dark, but it can't be all perfect, can it?"

"Definitely not. You like to write down takeaways, right? Here's another one for you: go for better, not for best."

TAKEAWAY 10

Go for better, not for best.

"You're saying that we shouldn't always strive to do better?" Martin asked.

"On the contrary, that's what I say: always try to do better. But do it in small steps, and never aim for perfection. Obsession with perfection kills all initiative and fun."

"Mmm." Martin waited a second. "I always thought strategy was about being the best and greatest. That's what I've been taught, and that's what you read in business books and magazines."

"Sure, but that doesn't necessarily make it true. Maybe it applies to giant corporations with CEOs who try to conquer the world and maximize their wealth, but for us it doesn't work. And I suspect that it's the same for many other normal companies like us—companies that are constantly working to smoothly run and improve their business."

"So you're saying that the high failure rates in strategy are because of too much focus on perfection?" Martin asked.

"It's definitely one of the reasons. But there are more. Let me give you another one, related but also different: death by planning."

"Death by planning?" Martin grabbed his pencil and paper to write down the next takeaway that was certainly coming.

"Yeah, death by planning. What I mean is that many companies pay too much attention to strategy analysis, trying to predict with as much certainty as possible where the world is heading. But that doesn't work, or even worse, it is harmful because it draws the attention away from what really matters in strategy."

"Why? How?"

"It doesn't work because the world is constantly changing and is too complex to understand anyway. There's simply a lot of uncertainty, making the past a bad predictor of the future."

"Okay, I get that, but you're saying that's harmful?"

"Of course! Imagine how much time is being spent on gathering data, crunching numbers, writing extensive reports, and so on! And imagine if all that time and effort would instead have been devoted to making solid, confident decisions and being proactive!"

Marina had raised her voice. *This is obviously something dear to her heart*, Martin thought. He wrote down what Marina said.

TAKEAWAY 11

Aim for confidence, decisions, and actions,
not for certainty, analysis, and prediction.

"And you're saying that," he began, pointing to his notes, "confidence, decisions, and actions are what we should really focus on. Decisions and actions I get, but confidence?"

"Confidence is key," Marina answered, "and much more important and achievable than certainty. Since strategy is about the future, everything is subjective and speculative. This makes people's sound judgments—and their confidence in whether we're making the right decisions and taking the right actions—a much more solid basis for strategy than so-called hard data."

Wow, she really cares about this stuff, Martin thought, listening to Marina's emphatic and passionate response.

"You really care about this stuff, right?"

"Yes. Because it's super important, and people just don't seem to get it. Of course, things like data, analysis, and strategy formulation are important. But there's so much more to strategy than just that. In the end, it is not the strategy itself that counts but what happens as a result. It's so obvious, but still people insist on wasting endless hours in data gathering, analysis, and prediction. I think that, in today's world, some of those big-company strategy reports are obsolete by the time they're published!"

"Why do you think companies do this?"

"I've thought about that a lot, but I don't really know. It's like a rain dance. We do it as some kind of ritual without asking whether or not it works. And of course," Marina added with a wry smile, "sometimes it actually rains, and everybody gleefully thinks their data analysis and predictions were perfectly correct!"

Interesting. Death by planning, strategic analysis as a rain dance— this Marina knows what she's talking about, Martin thought.

"Does that mean that, actually, good strategy is all about execution?" he asked.

"That's what they say, but no, that's actually not the solution. Until fifteen years ago or so, Waters & Flows was a company that focused almost exclusively on execution. While we were highly productive and efficient, we didn't look at the long term and hardly did any innovation. And it nearly killed us. That's because we had no strategy."

"So a company needs both?"

"Exactly! Strategy and execution are two sides of the same coin. You can't separate them. They are like yin and yang, highly intertwined and each one contains the seeds and starting point for the other."

"You need to explain that, but let me first write that down." Martin took his pencil and wrote:

TAKEAWAY 12

Treat strategy and execution as yin and yang.
You need both, and they are inextricably intertwined.

And below that he also drew a picture:

"Interesting—really interesting—I never thought about it this way. I always thought it was a linear process where you first spend a lot of time on formulating a strategy and then implement it."

"I totally understand. That's the traditional view, and that's how I looked at it for a long time as well. But not anymore. The whole yin-yang metaphor works very well, even if you dig into the philosophy behind it. But that's probably more for a long philosophical discussion over drinks," Marina laughed. "Anyway, the main point is that strategy and execution form a dynamic cycle that never starts or stops. While we execute our strategy, new Issues, Insights, and Ideas pop up that we then include in our strategy. And when we work on our strategy, we make new decisions and actions that guide our execution. You see, yin and yang, including the dots that you have drawn."

"I like this. To be frank, I always thought this whole yin-yang thing was a bit of Chinese hippie nonsense. But I think I'm starting to understand why my sister is constantly wearing her yin and yang necklace."

"Ah, that's why you can draw the sign so accurately, including the dots!"

"Yeah, I've seen it so often—and not just the necklace. She also has a large framed poster of it in her house, if you can believe it! But, as you said, that's probably more for a long discussion over drinks. Let's go back to strategy."

"Definitely. Is there anything else you want to know?"

"I actually came to ask you about the potential downsides of the One-Hour Strategy, but it seems so far we've talked more about the fundamentals, more about its strengths than about its weaknesses."

"Sorry about that, but as you've probably noticed by now, I am just so passionate about how we do strategy here and how I think many other companies could do it as well to improve their strategy success rates."

"That's totally fine, and I probably shouldn't ask you about weaknesses then. Maybe before I have to go, are there more fundamentals to the one-hour approach that we haven't talked about?"

"I think there is one more. You triggered a thought when

you mentioned about strengths and weakness. You know the SWOT, right?"

"Yes."

"Don't worry, I don't want to talk about that. But what it triggered for me is that, in our strategy, we focus more on what's going on inside our organization than on what's happening outside the company."

"I see. Why is that?"

"Of course, we shouldn't be naïve or blind to what is happening in our industry or in the world at large. That's why we have the 'M' of Momentum in our 6M Model. But there's so much! If you try to follow or pay attention to everything that could possibly affect your strategy—all of the potential outside influences, I mean—you get completely lost and confused."

"And that's why you focus on the inside, rather than the outside?" Martin pressed.

"Yes, but that's only half of the story. The other half is that strategy is all about finding a unique way to create value for customers. And this uniqueness lies inside, within our company. It's in our people, our processes, our culture, our history, our knowledge, and so on. Leveraging this uniqueness is what strategy is all about."

Martin looked for his pencil, which had gone missing. "Where is it?" He looked on the table, in his lap, and on the floor and saw it under his chair. After picking it up, he wrote:

TAKEAWAY 13

Start your strategy inside, and leverage
your company's uniqueness.

"You're completely right," Marina said, pointing at what Martin had written. "That's it," she concluded. "And now I'm afraid I'll have to let you go, because it's already five past the hour and my next appointment is waiting."

"Oh, sorry. But thanks a lot, really. This was a great meeting!"

Martin gratefully left Marina's office, his mind in something of a haze from all of the information that she had discussed with him. Happy to once again return to his "actual work" through the rest of the afternoon, he realized that he still hadn't heard anyone talk about the downsides of the One-Hour Strategy. What Marina had told him about the fundamentals was great, but still, there must be downsides, or challenges to the model, or even problems, too. If not Marina, who could he ask? He suddenly remembered that he hadn't had the chance yet to speak with Michelle about the One-Hour Strategy. If there was anyone in this company who could tell him the downsides, it would be Michelle.

"What Is" Questions

1. How much time does your company spend on strategy analysis and making plans compared to actual execution and implementation?

2. What is the effect of that? Do you recognize the "death by planning" problem?

3. What is the cause? Why do you think strategy formulation gets more attention (especially from the board) than strategy execution?

4. How much emphasis is there on external trends, predictions, opportunities, and threats in your company's strategy plans?

5. How much guidance do these really provide for establishing your company's strategy?

6. How well do you and others truly know your company's unique assets, competences, or DNA?

7. To what extent is that uniqueness the foundational core of your company's strategy?

"What If" Questions

1. What would be the effect if strategy execution were taken just as seriously in your company as strategy generation?

2. How would it benefit your company if strategy generation and execution were combined into one coherent and continuous process?

3. What would it take to create such combined process? How can you use the tools provided in the previous chapters?

4. How would it benefit your company's strategy if everyone emphasized your company's unique assets, competences, and DNA as its foundation?

5. Thinking about it, how would your company perform if it would successfully leverage its unique assets to serve customers and stand out from key competitors?

6. Can you see how putting development and change ("better") center stage is more productive than focusing on end results ("best")?

7. How would your company benefit if strategy making focused more on confidence in concrete decisions and actions and less on conceptual analysis and prediction?

CHAPTER 7

ONE-HOUR
STRATEGY PITFALLS

THE NEXT DAY AT WORK, Martin immediately went to Michelle. "Hey, Michelle, can I ask you some questions about the One-Hour Strategy?"

"Why me?" she responded immediately, as if Martin had singled her out for some strange reason. "Why don't you ask Marina? She's the expert, and I'm rather busy right at the moment."

"I know, but that's why I want to talk to you. I talked to Marina, and she is so excited about the One-Hour Strategy that she can only talk about the bright side. I want to know whether there are downsides. And besides, I had wanted to talk to you about the One-Hour Strategy already anyway during our online meeting last week."

"Oh, I see. So you're asking me because I'm the skeptic of the team. Is that it?" Michelle was still quite aggressive.

"Well . . . kind of . . . not exactly. But, since the day I started working here, you've already said a lot of smart, innovative things about how we could improve our marketing and sales funnel. My thinking was, or is, that because you are so keenly focused on improvements, then you must be aware of any, let's say, shortcomings of the One-Hour Strategy—things that some of your improvement ideas are aimed at fixing. So I thought . . ."

"Okay, I have ten minutes. What do you want to know?"

"May we go to the conference room so as to not disturb the rest?"

"Sure, if you want to."

While they walked there, Martin explained, "The whole One-Hour Strategy thing makes a lot of sense to me, and I like everything I have heard: 6M, the three questions, the 3Is, yin and yang . . ."

"Yin and yang? You *have* talked to Marina!"

"Yes?"

"She always brings in Chinese philosophy to make a point. It's not bad, and it does match the one-hour approach, but I prefer to keep things more down-to-earth, more pragmatic and practical, if you will," Michelle replied.

"Great, that's why I want to talk to you," Martin said, his tone becoming serious. They were in the conference room now. "Can we be perfectly honest and open here? If the One-Hour Strategy were all sweetness and light, every company out there would be doing it, and Waters & Flows would not be the uniquely managed company that it is. I'm also of the impression that almost every business model or program that is truly effective in making a given company successful is difficult; that is to say, successful models or programs take a lot of work to implement and conscious effort to maintain. So that is why I want to know, in your objective view—your practical view, as you say—what are some of the pitfalls of the approach?"

"Well said," Michelle replied. "There are three," she continued, while raising three fingers, as if she had already prepared a presentation about this. "One, it takes a lot of time and persistence to implement it. Two, it focuses mostly on incremental improvements. And three, it requires constant attention to keep it alive. That's it. Any further questions?"

"Well, that's a bit of a short answer. Could you expand a little more?"

"They are pretty obvious, but since you're new, I'll go slow."

"Thanks." Martin didn't really understand why, but he was starting to like Michelle's directness.

"The first pitfall is to underestimate the change of paradigm that the One-Hour Strategy is. While it is simple in itself and truly makes good sense once you get it, it is so different from what people are used to and have learned from conventional strategy textbooks and education that they have a hard time accepting it."

"I can imagine. Initially I found the basic concept intriguing, and it's part of the reason I came to Waters & Flows. But I had the same reaction when I learned more about it when I started here last week. When you hear it for the first time, it sounds exotic and strange, and it's kind of a difficult transition in practical terms. And nothing at all like what I learned getting my MBA," Martin replied.

"Exactly. Everyone has that same feeling. But once you understand the One-Hour Strategy, you can't imagine you ever thought differently about strategy, because it feels so natural and self-evident. Before you get to that point, however, it's easy to reject the whole idea and laugh about it. As the expression goes, you have to win over people's hearts and minds to what for them is a whole new conceptualization."

"So the first pitfall is that the One-Hour Strategy doesn't come easy?"

"Something like that. I'd rather say that this particular pitfall arises only if you don't persist long and hard enough."

"Me?"

"Of course not. I mean as a company. If you want to implement the One-Hour Strategy, you need a lot of patience and persistence. And not just anyone's patience and persistence. You need a convinced person with strong commitment at the highest level in the organization."

"So would you say that companies shouldn't bother starting to implement the One-Hour Strategy unless at least one of their executives strongly believes in it and is willing to put in a lot of effort to make it work?"

"Yes, finally, you get it! Thank you!" Michelle almost shouted while raising both hands.

Not knowing whether he should feel offended or whether this was actually a Michelle-style compliment, Martin wrote down his next takeaway.

TAKEAWAY 14

Only adopt the One-Hour Strategy if
at least one executive strongly believes in it.

"Okay, that's one. The second pitfall is that, while the One-Hour Strategy is strong at incremental changes, it is not so strong at more radical, large-scale changes to strategy," Michelle continued.

"And you would say we need both?" Martin asked.

"Not just me. Research on innovation shows this as well. Incremental changes are most important and should be frequent. They reflect how strategy should normally be updated. It's like driving a car—you have to adjust your speed and braking based on things like traffic, or pedestrians, or terrain, or weather conditions. Companies shouldn't radically change their course frequently. They should nurture where they come from and what they have built up, and the incremental approach of the One-Hour Strategy works very well with that."

"But?" Martin filled in what Michelle was going to say.

"But, every now and then, a company needs to make a more radical change. Sometimes things need to be shaken up and a new course must be taken."

"For example, when a new technology has taken over the old one?"

"Indeed, or when a product has reached its end-of-life stage, or the competition has changed substantially, or a crisis happens, or any other reason why the company can't simply continue along the same path it has taken before."

"And the One-Hour Strategy can't help you with that?" Martin asked.

"It can, but it doesn't come naturally. The whole idea of the One-Hour Strategy still works. After all, it doesn't exclude radical change. Anyone can bring in whatever issue, insight, or idea, no matter how radical. But the truth is that this rarely happens. People are good at thinking in terms of incremental changes across all 6Ms, but they are usually not good at big-picture thinking that encompasses the whole or in coming up with radical ideas and opportunities."

"Is there a solution to this pitfall?" Martin asked.

"There is. Because we had observed this problem for a

number of years in a row, we added a new element to the one-hour approach three years ago: Disruption Day."

"Disruption Day?"

"Yeah. It's not an exclusive part of the one-hour approach, but it's a great addition. It's based on an idea by a company called Atlassian. They called it FedEx Day, but that term didn't really fly here. We wanted something more original—a term that we coined for ourselves."

"FedEx Day? As in the delivery company?"

"Indeed. Atlassian called it that because the concept goal is to deliver innovations within twenty-four hours or less. They also call it ShipIt Day."

"Interesting! How does that work?"

"The idea is simple: We give our people one day of complete autonomy to work on anything that is not part of their regular job. The only requirement is that, at the end of that day, they show their results to the rest of the company."

"Fascinating. But complete autonomy? I'm sure that's not what you mean. People need guidance and a clear assignment, right?"

"No, they don't. That's another one of those beliefs that many people hold strongly but that just isn't correct," Michelle replied fiercely.

"Oh, sorry, I didn't mean to offend you. It's just—it's hard to believe."

"Yeah, my apologies, I get rather irritated when people believe things that are so obviously not true. But people can't help it; it's what they have been conditioned to believe. But the research is very clear: giving people autonomy is one of the greatest motivators for achieving extraordinary results."

"And extraordinary is what we want this time!" Martin added.

"Indeed. While, normally, strategy should be part of people's ordinary work, Disruption Day is extraordinary."

"How does it work? Can you give me more details?" Martin asked.

"Sure. Let me get the Disruption Day outline." Michelle opened her bag and without any hesitation took out a sheet of paper.

Of course, she's that *organized; why would I expect anything else?* Martin thought.

"Here it is."

DISRUPTION DAY OUTLINE

1. Schedule it at least six months in advance, and make sure it is blocked in everyone's calendar.

2. Assign an organizer or organizing team who is in charge of planning and running the day.

3. Organize a kickoff two weeks in advance to explain what is expected from everyone and let people create teams around possible ideas.

4. Start at 7 a.m. with breakfast, and let teams pitch what they will be working on.

5. Give teams from 8 a.m. to 8 p.m. to work on their disruption and create some sort of demo.

6. Provide everything they need during the day: food, drinks, paper, tools, etc.

7. Foster a relaxed, fun, and competitive atmosphere, not taking it too seriously.

8. Let people present their disruptions in five minutes over dinner, from 8 p.m. to 10 p.m.

9. Close the day with drinks and a celebration.

10. Harvest Issues, Insights, and Ideas during the next monthly Strategy Dialogue.

Martin had a look at the sheet. "The first two points are obvious. You need someone to lead the day, and you need to schedule it far ahead. Clear."

"Correct. The interesting part starts at the third point,"

Michelle replied. "To make sure people spend their time during Disruption Day in the best possible way, we do a kickoff two weeks in advance. The main point is to explain what the day looks like, why we do it, and what we expect from people. It is also the time to create teams. And since it's an extraordinary day and we want cross-disciplinary teams, they cannot work with more than one person from their own department."

"So they can choose teammates themselves, as long as they come from other departments?"

"Yes. Since we've been doing this for a couple of years now, most people already start creating their team way earlier, sometimes months before."

"Fascinating how motivated they are," Martin observed.

"It is, and it shows the enormous power of giving people autonomy. But let's move on to the actual day, since I only have about five minutes left to talk to you."

"Okay!"

"The day starts at 7 a.m. with a breakfast session. We serve everyone a rich breakfast with everything they can imagine, again to stress how extraordinary the day is. And during breakfast each team pitches their idea in thirty seconds max. They can still radically change their idea during the day, but this makes sure that everyone comes to the event prepared with at least some fundamental ideas or concepts. And you also feel the competition starting then."

"At 8 a.m. we ring a bell and announce the start of the twelve hours of work ahead. To keep the pressure high, we do the same every hour, telling them how much time they still have left."

"And they need to create a demo?"

"Yes, they need to produce something they can show. It can't be just a slide with bullets or an explanation. It needs to be something visual, tangible, or entertaining. It can be a video, a paper prototype, an app mock-up, anything."

"Great, I like that." Martin looked at his watch. "Items 6 and 7 I get. You want it to stay a special day with the right mood."

"Correct." Michelle nodded.

"And the presentations during dinner I also get."

"Yeah. At 8 p.m. the final bell rings, and everybody needs to drop their work and come to the lobby. There we've created a stage where each team presents their demo in five minutes max. I like this part of the day most. You really get surprised about what people have come up with in just twelve hours!"

That's the first time I've seen her excited, Martin thought. "I assume there is a lot of cheering and clapping?" he asked.

"There is. It's really cool. And in the meantime, we serve pizza. It's total chaos, which I normally hate. But it's a good chaos. It just needs to be like that."

"And then there's drinks," Martin added, nodding his head approvingly at the sheet of paper. "Makes sense, but what about the last part, item 10?"

"As I mentioned, we do these days for a reason. We want people to come up with disruptive issues, insights, and ideas for our strategy. To make sure things don't stop when people leave the office at midnight, we follow up during the next normal monthly Strategy Dialogue. This way, we incorporate the results of the extraordinary Disruption Day into our normal strategy process."

"And that closes the circle!" Martin shouted, feeling truly energized.

"It does." Now Michelle looked at her watch. "I just have two minutes left, so let me quickly explain the third pitfall to you, too."

"Yes, please! Is it as exciting as this one?"

"I'm afraid not. It's actually the boring side of things, and it's probably the biggest pitfall of all of them: losing focus. The One-Hour Strategy requires constant attention to keep it alive."

"Isn't that true for everything?" Martin asked.

"It is. If you stop putting energy into the one-hour approach, it stops, and people go back to business as usual, only focused on their day-to-day work. This is a well-known problem in strategy execution and not limited to the one-hour approach. In fact, the whole one-hour approach was largely developed *specifically* to solve this problem: by making strategy the rule, having everyone involved, and so on, it becomes something natural for the company. But this doesn't mean it goes on automatically. That's a myth. It's just an insidious force of nature: anything that deviates from the path—and we're doing this to constantly update and reinvigorate our path—requires energy. So does the One-Hour Strategy. This is why we have Marina."

"The One-Hour Strategy expert?" Martin replied.

"She's the expert, indeed. But more than anything else, she's the person who keeps things going, who reminds people, who exhorts everyone for results, progress, issues, and so on. She's definitely our One-Hour Strategy *engine*. And the company facilitates her. This is an important part of her job, so she gets all the time and resources she needs to manage the process."

"And without her, the whole thing would fall apart?"

"Most certainly. It might survive for a while, and even longer at some places in the company because some colleagues are very active, too. But in the end, it would stop working; it would just grind to a halt. Because it only works if it is done company-wide, and this requires everyone to participate to some degree or another. But now I have to run." In an instant, Michelle was gone, right out the door.

"Thank you!" Martin shouted, but she had already disappeared around the corner. In the meantime, he had written down his next takeaway.

TAKEAWAY 15

Allocate resources and make someone responsible for the One-Hour Strategy.

"That's it," he mumbled to himself. "That's the One-Hour Strategy. It's not perfect and there are pitfalls, but it's certainly the most interesting and sensible approach to strategy that I've ever seen. Quite remarkable."

Martin closed the door of the conference room and went back to his office, where he spent the rest of the day working on the marketing plan for an important client.

SELF-EVALUATION

"What Is" Questions

1. In your company or organization, do people get enough time to spend on strategy and execution? Or is it just something they need to do on the side?

2. Are sufficient budgets allocated? Have money and other resources been made available for executing the strategy? If not, what is the effect of that?

3. Who, if anyone, is responsible for strategy execution in your company? And for keeping abreast of developments that may affect the strategy?

4. Does the top leadership team of your company spend enough time and effort on making sure the strategy gets executed? If not, what is the impact of that?

5. Is there enough out-of-the-box thinking and radical, free-form ideas generated by people in your company? Or are most people stuck in how things are normally done?

6. If not, what is the consequence of that? How does it limit your company's ability to change and keep up with developments in your industry and in the world?

7. Is there someone at the board level who has the willingness, power, ability, and persistence to change the way strategy is done in your company?

"What If" Questions

1. How would strategy execution in your company improve if people actually got the time and resources to do what is needed?

2. Suppose one of your company's executives stands up and says, "We're going to adopt this One-Hour Strategy method." Who would that person be?

3. What can you personally do to make this happen? How can you help, and what would you need to get the process started?

4. What would happen if one or more people in your company took on the responsibility of managing the entire strategy process? Who could that be?

5. What effect could a yearly Disruption Day have on your company? How many novel and usable ideas do you think it would generate?

6. How would you organize a Disruption Day? When should it take place? What might you be able to do today to put this in motion?

7. How could the core idea of the One-Hour Strategy—putting strategy into the hands of many people company-wide—be extended to other processes in the company?

CHAPTER 8

FROM ONE-HOUR THEORY TO PRACTICE

IT WAS FRIDAY, THE LAST DAY of Martin's second week at Waters & Flows. Over the past two weeks, Martin had heard a lot of theory about the One-Hour Strategy. He learned all the principles and tools and had written down no less than fifteen takeaways, so far. It all made a lot of sense to him, and he thought he understood it quite well. It was a new way of thinking about strategy making, but ultimately, it simply added up.

But still, he hadn't seen any examples yet. It wasn't hard at all to imagine, for instance, what the answers to the three questions of Relevance, Progress, and Mood could look like, or what a 6M Model filled with Issues, Insights, and Ideas would look like. However, Martin reasoned that some practical, boots-on-the-ground examples of the One-Hour Strategy in operation would be very insightful. It would show him not simply how the strategy looks but how it feels and how it works.

Who could I ask? he thought. *Probably Marina, but I've already taken so much of her time, I don't want to bother her again. And Alex will be too busy, and* I don't *dare to ask Michelle again . . .*

But then he suddenly realized that Marina had told him that there were three big reasons why strategy should be part of everybody's job. She had given him only two so far and had promised to explain the third reason to him at a later time. So he decided that this presented another convenient opportunity to talk to Marina again. After all, he wanted to get the whole picture.

After starting his morning with some work for a client, he knocked on Marina's door at 10:47 a.m. "Marina, sorry to disturb you once again, but can I ask you two more questions about the One-Hour Strategy?"

"Of course. You can always ask me. That's what I'm here for!"

"Well, I remember that you said there were three big reasons why strategy should be part of everyone's job, or why everyone should be involved in strategy making."

"Indeed," Marina replied.

"The first two you have explained. First, it leads to better strategy because you're including a lot of different viewpoints, and together people know more than any person could know on their own, correct?"

Marina nodded.

"Second, it also leads to smoother execution because people feel more committed because it's their strategy, or at least a tiny part of it is theirs, right?"

"You're right."

"But what is the third reason? I had forgotten about it, but I suddenly remembered you wanted to tell me later."

"Of course!" Marina smiled. "Well, the third big reason is that it allows us to develop and enhance our strategic competence as a company. Because everyone is involved and works on our strategy one hour per day, per week, or per month, based on their position, everyone in our company learns to think and act more strategically."

"So it's a kind of learning?" Martin asked.

"One hundred percent. It's kind of an *ongoing* learning process. People learn by doing. Not from a book, or a theory, or a lecture, but from practicing the one-hour approach regularly and repeatedly. And in this way, we as a company, and each employee individually, become better and more proficient at it. In other words, we're building a company of strategic thinkers."

"Perfect," Martin replied. "I like that. A company of strategic thinkers. And your answer brings me immediately to my second question, since you're talking about theory and practice. So far, I've mainly learned the theory of the one-hour approach, but I still haven't seen it work in practice."

"You most certainly will during your next monthly One-Hour Strategy Dialogue."

"I know, but that's not until Tuesday of next week. In the meantime, do you perhaps have an example that demonstrates the one-hour approach in practice?"

"Didn't you already get those in your welcome package?"

"I don't think so," Martin replied.

"The blue envelope?"

Shoot! Suddenly, Martin blushed as he remembered he hadn't opened that particular envelope. It was still at home, sitting on his desk. *How could I not have looked at it?*

"Anyway, I'll show you an example." Marina reached behind her to grab a sheet of paper.

"Here's a 6M Model from a monthly One-Hour Strategy Dialogue the production department held a year ago. Have a look."

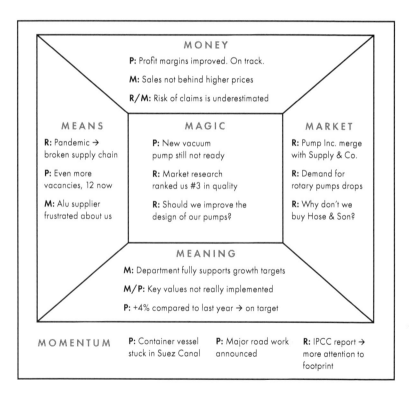

Martin had a close look at the sheet. "Interesting," he said. "What's interesting?"

"The whole thing, but in particular, I notice that there are three things listed for each M. Is that a coincidence?"

"No, that's on purpose. Even though it's not a strict rule, we've noticed that having more than three Issues, Insights, or Ideas for any of the 6Ms becomes hard to process. Of course, if needed, they should be added, but it's a good rule of thumb to stay focused."

"Let me write that down," Martin said.

> **TAKEAWAY 16**
>
> As a rule of thumb, focus on no more than three Issues, Insights, and Ideas per M.

"And now that you mention Issues, Insights, or Ideas, I don't recognize them in the model."

"You're right, and that also is on purpose. In the end, it doesn't really matter whether something is an Issue, an Insight, or an Idea. What matters is that it gets on the table. What you see in this example is a mix of all three. The ideas are usually easiest to recognize because they end with a question mark."

"Like 'Should we improve the design of our pumps?'"

"Correct. One of our engineers brought this in. His son works at Apple and always makes fun of how ugly the products are that his father works on. And he has a point. Design has never been a big deal in our market, but we have noticed in recent years that customers are becoming more sensitive to it. Do you see something else that you find remarkable?" Marina asked.

"Not really. It looks quite logical to me, and I can see how this is the result of a monthly session with production."

"What I mean," Marina continued, "is that the model mentions only the things that matter. It is not at all a complete description of production along the 6Ms."

"So it's not really production's strategy but more a snapshot of what requires attention?"

"That's what it is. We don't need a complete description. What we need to know at any particular point in time is what to focus our attention on in the next period. That makes it a very action-oriented approach to strategy."

"I want to write that one down too!" Martin said.

TAKEAWAY 17

Don't describe a complete strategy.
Focus on what requires attention next.

He looked again at the model. "I see that sales is not in favor of the higher prices? That's my department!"

"Because raw materials prices have increased substantially, and wages have risen as well, we had no choice but to increase our prices by about 10 percent or so. Sales didn't like that because it would make their job harder. But there was no way around it."

"And why is this in the strategy of production?"

"Because it affects them as well. As you can see from the M before it, it's a Mood thing. The relationship between production and sales is always difficult, and the fact that it shows up here is good news. It shows that the people in production are aware of this."

"Which reduces silo thinking," Martin added.

Marina nodded.

"And why are there an R and an M before 'Risk of claims is underestimated'?" Martin asked.

"Because it's both a Relevance and a Mood thing. The M refers to the fact that the awareness of the risk of claims is pretty low throughout this company. Historically the threat of lawsuits was never really a big deal, but it happens more and more often now. In other words, risk of claims carries a higher relevance these days. At the same time, our people need to be more consciously attuned to that higher potential."

"So the R means that this may affect your overall strategy as well, when moving forward," Martin added again.

"Correct. You seem to get it."

"One more question. I can vividly see how this is the result of a monthly dialogue session. But what happens afterward? After all, it's nice to have this on paper, but something needs to be done, right? Some relevant action needs to be taken?"

"It certainly does. Someone explained to you the agenda of the dialogue sessions, right?"

"Yeah, Gunther. Believe it or not, I remember the breakdown of the hour into the 2-10-20-20-8-minute schedule. Oh wait, the eight minutes was for actions, I believe."

"Correct. At the end of the meeting, the team defines the most important actions to take. Of course, that's not enough, but it shows how we immediately make the transition to strategy execution during that same meeting. Based on this particular monthly dialogue session, we decided to hire our first designer from art school; we raised prices less than originally planned after consulting with sales; and we started working with two new suppliers in response to the container ship stuck in the Suez Canal, as well as other pandemic-related supply chain breakdowns. We took several other steps, but these examples show you how the monthly dialogue sessions truly drive action."

"And look," Marina said, pointing at something she had written on her whiteboard. Martin copied it down.

> **TAKEAWAY 18**
>
> Always end with actions, because
> without actions, nothing ever changes.

"So every meeting ends with actions?"

"Every meeting ends with actions. And that doesn't just go for meetings. Also, when an executive or a manager works on their strategy on their own, they should always turn whatever they have done into actions, because—"

Martin jumped in and finished her statement: "—without actions, nothing ever changes."

The End

SELF-EVALUATION

"What Is" Questions

1. Why do you think the idea that strategy should be high-level and abstract (because making it concrete would put it into the realm of the operational) might be flawed?

2. If your company has a previously developed strategic plan, how viable and alive is it in practice? Is it up-to-date and driving day-to-day work?

3. How well does it describe the difference between the status quo and where the company wants to be? What happens if this difference is not clear to people?

4. How often are resources and attention allocated too thinly across too many initiatives in your company? How has such lack of focus affected performance?

5. How is your own work affected by this? How is a lack of clarity and focus in the company's strategic direction affecting your work?

6. Does the organizational unit you are working for have its own strategy, derived from the company's overall strategy? If not, how does it hinder you?

7. How actionable is your company's strategy? Are ambitions and goals translated into clear actions? If not, what is the effect of that?

"What If" Questions

1. How would it help your company if it always focused on the things that should have most priority?

2. Spend one hour filling out the 6M Model for the organizational unit you are working for. What does it look like?

3. Which issues, insights, and ideas can you identify? What kinds of actions would be needed to address them?

4. Suppose the One-Hour Strategy was adopted in your company. What would it look like? What would be different from today?

5. What would be the effect? How would your company benefit? How would your employees benefit? How would you benefit?

6. What would be the first thing you could do today to start embracing the One-Hour Strategy as the strategy approach for your company?

7. What would you need to make it happen? Who should be involved, what support would you need, and who besides yourself can you enlist to provide this?

CHAPTER 9

WHAT THE ONE-HOUR STRATEGY MEANS FOR YOU

BACK TO YOU. You've now seen how Waters & Flows has embraced strategy as a core process throughout all levels and roles in the company using the One-Hour Strategy approach.

I am going to guess that you are quite surprised about what you read and that you haven't worked for any organization doing strategy in this way. And maybe you even feel that the One-Hour Strategy approach doesn't look very *strategic* in the first place.

You would be entirely right, because that's the point. Done well, strategy is not something mystical reserved for the top of the organization. Strategy is for everyone and must come from everyone. It is a down-to-earth business process that belongs to everyone's day-to-day job. Stated differently, proactive strategy making is integral to everyone's day-to-day job.

My intention with this book is to inspire you and open your mind to this alternative approach to strategy that, however unconventional, is a more viable approach than the traditional top-down, analytical approach to strategy that appears in conventional business textbooks and is routinely taught in MBA programs.

The One-Hour Strategy approach is not meant as a strict set of rules to follow; nor is it the ultimate final version of how strategy should be done. It's a beginning, a source of inspiration, a seed for doing things differently. Therefore, you don't need to adopt the approach literally as it is outlined in this story. Feel free to adapt it and improve it so that it matches your organization's culture, mission, and long-term goals. This adaptability is key and something that I strongly encourage among the many companies I work with or advise.

Waters & Flows is imagined as a midsize three-level company with executives, managers, and employees. Maybe your organization is a large, multilayered corporation, a small firm or entrepreneurial startup with a handful of partners all wearing many hats, or a nonprofit. Or maybe your company is just you, wearing *all* the hats!

The basics of the One-Hour Strategy approach apply to all these organizations. The main difference in adopting the approach is deciding who should be spending how much time on strategy. If it's just you, or if you're with a handful of people, you're most like a strategy executive, meaning that you should probably be spending one hour per day on strategy, or maybe one hour every two days. If you're a small firm with two instead of three levels, it mostly makes sense to simply remove the manager level from the approach and focus on what executives and employees should do. And if you're working for a large or very large company, you may want to introduce additional One-Hour Strategy levels in between executives and managers or in between managers and employees and adjust the approach accordingly.

Waters & Flows, as it is described in our story, is a relatively traditional company with a hierarchical organizational structure. Maybe your organization is more decentralized, works with self-managing teams, or has adopted contemporary ways of organizing, such as the so-called agile practices, flatarchy, or holacracy.

In that case, the distinction between executives, managers, and employees is less evident, and the balance between who is spending how much time on strategy is likely very different from the conventional. Nevertheless, the basics of the One-Hour Strategy still apply—potentially even more so than in a traditional company. Because, like these more decentralized ways of organizing, the One-Hour Strategy puts strategy in the hands of all employees instead of keeping it the responsibility of a selected few.

Whatever your organization looks like, I'm convinced you will find a way to adapt the one-hour approach to make it fit. Figuring that out isn't the main challenge. As with strategy, it is not the ideas or plans that are most challenging. It's the implementation of those ideas and plans that is most crucial. Conceiving how the one-hour approach would work for your company is relatively easy, and this book should give you a head start. Implementing the approach can be a challenge, however. Not because it is difficult, or complex, or expensive. It's because it doesn't match the firmly held conventional wisdom about how strategy ought to be done. Therefore, your main barriers will be psychological. In effect, it will be a matter of fighting the "We've always done it this way" mentality.

Accordingly, embracing the One-Hour Strategy requires a substantial shift in people's mindset. This takes time and persistence. Therefore, give it time, be patient, and persist until your organization can reap the benefits and achieve extraordinary everyday success as a company of truly strategic thinkers.

The following table is a summary of the key takeaways and their reasoning. For additional information and materials, visit www.theonehourstrategy.com.

TAKEAWAY	REASON
1. Make strategy the rule, not the exception.	In a world in flux, strategy is the only thing that can give a company the stability it needs.
2. Make strategy part of everyone's job.	Only when it is a part of people's ordinary jobs can strategy truly drive behavior.
3. When complexity increases, involve more people.	Strategy is complex by nature. Including more perspectives means better decisions.
4. In making strategy, pay attention to the details.	It is details that make a strategy unique and guide execution.
5. Make strategy a continuous process, not an event.	Everything in a successfully functioning company is continuous. Strategy needs to align with that.
6. Make strategy internally, within your own offices and meeting rooms.	Going elsewhere creates an unwanted physical and a symbolic distance, as well as the potential for distraction.

7. Monitor actively; change reluctantly.

Strategy creates necessary stability, but it must be swiftly adapted once the need for change is evident.

8. Everyone works at strategy at their own level and from their own perspective.

No one knows everything, and everyone knows something. Only together can people successfully create the company's strategy.

9. Internalize the 6M Model and the three questions and keep them front of mind, always.

Change often comes unexpectedly, even creatively. You want to be always prepared to recognize innovative ideas.

10. Go for better, not for best.

An obsession with perfection paralyzes people and blocks action. A continuous focus on improvement drives action.

11. Aim for confidence, decisions, and actions, not for certainty, analysis, and prediction.

Strategy is about creating the future. It is always uncertain and subjective. Data is about the past and may therefore be irrelevant.

12. Treat strategy and execution as yin and yang. You need both, and they are inextricably intertwined.

Strategy and execution are two sides of one and the same process. Neither happens effectively without the other.

13. Start your strategy inside, and leverage your company's uniqueness.

Your assets and skills are your only reliable anchor for strategy; the rest is in flux.

14. Only adopt the One-Hour Strategy if at least one executive strongly believes in it.

Without a powerful and persistent leader, the paradigm change of the One-Hour Strategy simply will not take off.

15. Allocate resources and make someone responsible for the One-Hour Strategy.

Strategy and execution require serious and constant dedicated resources and attention.

16. As a rule of thumb, focus on no more than three Issues, Insights, and Ideas per M.

When resources and attention are spread too thinly, nothing happens.

17. Don't describe a complete strategy. Focus on what requires attention next.

What matters is not the end point. It is the change that is put in motion. Effective strategy, in the long term, is essentially a moving target.

18. Always end with actions because without actions, nothing ever changes.

The end goal of any given strategy is not the strategy itself; it is the actual implementation of action.

ABOUT THE AUTHOR

 **JEROEN KRAAIJENBRINK** is an accomplished strategy educator, speaker, writer, and consultant with over two decades of experience, extending from academia through modern business and industry. He empowers people and organizations to discover, formulate, and execute their future plans by providing innovative tools for expansive and forward-thinking strategy making and both personal and organizational development. In doing so, he enables individuals to realize their greatest ambitions and organizations to effectively achieve their business goals and mission through ongoing, effective strategy techniques.

Drawing from cognitive psychology, humanism, martial arts, Saint Benedict, and an extraordinarily wide range of other sources, he has written innumerable articles on strategy, sustainability, and personal leadership, as well as authored four books: *Strategy Consulting*, *No More Bananas*, *Unlearning Strategy*, and *The Strategy Handbook*. He is an active contributor to *Forbes*, where he writes about strategy, leadership, and how to embrace and harness the complexity and uncertainty—and the opportunities—of the global marketplace that the world has become.

He has a PhD in industrial management, teaches strategy at the University of Amsterdam Business School, and has helped significantly improve the strategic planning of many midsize and larger companies across the engineering, manufacturing, healthcare, and financial services industries.

Printed in Great Britain
by Amazon

33616192R00070